Copyri

MW01025443

NORW.

compiled and edited
by E.C. "Red" Stangland

Published by

NORSE PRESS

Box 1554
Sioux Falls, SD 57101
U.S.A.

Illustrated by
Don Steinbeck

19TH PRINTING
ISBN 0-9602692-0-7

Ethnic jokes are a traditional way to relieve tension. When people laugh at each other as well as at themselves, built-up tensions have a way of disappearing.

True, an ethnic joke has a way of appearing cruel and heartless. Certain ethnic groups take great exception to them. Over the years we have had Pat and Mike stories, Rastus jokes, Scotchmen jokes. In recent times, Canadians have generated millions of laughs with "Newfie Jokes" about Newfoundlanders. Sooner or later, we all get a chance to be the dunce. It would appear that telling jokes on one another is far more desirable than shooting and bombing each other over cultural and religious differences.

We have been publishing this book of Norwegian Jokes for ten years with over a half million printed. In all this time we have had less than ten complaints. In most cases, the objection was not as much about the Norwegian theme as it was the somewhat earthy content of some of the jokes.

What we have learned in ten years is that Norwegians love to laugh at themselves. They have enough self-image to not take the jokes personally. We have seen these jokes serve as ice-breakers and therapeutic laugh stimulators throughout the U.S. and Canada. In fact, we get mail orders from all over the world.

So, if you are lucky enough to be of Norwegian descent, we are confident you will thoroughly enjoy the crazy Ole & Lena stories. If you come from another ethnic background, feel free to laugh as loudly as you wish because we Norskies will be laughing right along with you.

Laughingly yours,
E.C. "Red" Stangland, Publisher

A Norwegian went on an elephant hunt, but was forced to turn back because he developed a hernia from carrying the decoy.

A Norwegian girl considered getting an abortion because she didn't think the baby was hers.

How do you hide money from a Norwegian?
Place it under a soap dish.

A Norwegian went to his Doctor for a physical, complaining about his sex life. The Doc told him to walk ten miles a day, then call him on the phone. A week later, the Norwegian telephoned his Doctor. "How's your sex life," inquired the Doc. "What sex?" blurted the Norwegian. "I'm seventy miles from home."

Why is there always a garbage can present at a Norwegian wedding?
To keep the flies off the bride.

Norwegian (working a crossword puzzle): What's a four-letter word ending in 'it' for something that lies on the bottom of a bird cage?
Swede: Grit.
Norwegian: Would you mind if I borrowed your eraser?

The Norwegians in Minneapolis have come up with a new drink. They mix Tang and prune juice . . . and call it "Prune Tang."

Why did the Norwegian freeze to death?
Because he went to the drive-in movie to see "Closed for the Winter."

Difference between "Uff Da" and "Fee Da:"
Uff Da . . . dropping a sack of garbage.
Fee Da . . . getting your hand in it.

Norwegian plumber's dream: Fixing Farrah's Fawcett . . . or Olivia Newton's John.

Two Norwegians dressed a hog in overalls and placed it between them in their pick-up truck as they crossed a Swedish border. Their motive was to avoid paying a special livestock tax. The border guard eyed the trio, asking their names. "Ole Johnson." "Knute Johnson." Then, the hog: "Oink." Passing them on, the guard remarked to his assistant, "I've seen some bad looking people in my time, but that Oink Johnson has got to be the ugliest Norwegian I've ever seen."

What did the Norwegian call his pet Zebra?
"Spot."

How did the Norwegian get pregnant?
He went out with a telephone operator and she reversed the charge.

A Norwegian nurse was asked why she had a rectal thermometer behind her ear.
"My goodness," she exclaimed, "now I remember where I mislaid that ballpoint pen."

NORWEGIAN MEDICAL DICTIONARY

Anally – Occurring yearly

Artery – Study of paintings

Bacteria – Back door to cafeteria

Barium – What doctors do when treatment fails

Bowel – Letter like A, E, I, O, U

Caesarian section – A district in Rome

Catarrh – Stringed instrument

Cat Scan – Searching for kitty

Cauterize – Made eye contact with her

Colic – A sheep dog

Coma – A punctuation mark

Congenital – Friendly

D & C — Where Washington is

Diarrhea – Journal of daily events

Dilate – To live long

Enema – Not a friend

Fester – Quicker

Fibula – Small lie

Genital – Non-Jewish

G.I Series – Soldiers' ball game

Grippe – Suitcase

Hangnail – Coat Hook

High Colonic – Jewish religious holiday

Impotent – Distinguished; well known

Intense pain – Torture in the tepee

Labor pain – Getting hurt at work

Medical staff – Doctor's cane

Morbid – Higher offer

Nitrate – Cheaper than day rate

Node – Was aware of

Outpatient – Person who has fainted

Pap Smear – Fatherhood test

Pelvis – Cousin of Elvis

Post operative – Letter carrier

Prostate – Flat on your back

Protein – Favoring young people

Recovering Room – Place to do upholstery

Rectum – Dang near killed 'em

Rheumatic – Amorous

Scar – Rolled tobacco leaf

Secretion – Hiding anything

Seizure – Roman Emperor

Serology – Study of Knighthood

Tablet – Small table

Terminal illness – Sickness at the airport

Tibia – Country in N. Africa

Tumor – An extra pair

Urine – Opposite of "you're out"

Varicose – Located nearby

Vein – Conceited

So, THAT'S the difference between Danes and Norwegians?

Ole and Lena got married. On their honeymoon trip, they were nearing Minneapolis when Ole put his hand on Lena's knee. Giggling, Lena said, "Ole, you can go farther if you vant to." So Ole drove on to Duluth.

At a fancy party, how can you identify the Norwegian?
He's the one with the yellow tennis shoes and the rusty zipper.

There's a new Norwegian drink that is becoming popular, a mixture of vodka and prune juice. It's called a "Pile Driver."

What do you find on the bottom of cola bottles in Norway?
The inscription "Open other end."

Ole the Norwegian loved his wife, Lena . . . even though she was a bad cook and left the food on the burner too long. When she finally presented Ole with a new baby, everyone in town held their breath when it was learned the baby had a rather dusky skin. But that didn't bother Ole. He just smiled and said, "Yah, dat Lena . . . she just burns everything."

Two Norwegians were sent up in a space capsule. During the flight, one of them went on a scheduled space walk outside the capsule. During the space walk, the door accidentally closed. So the Norwegian inside the capsule suddenly heard a rapping on the door. "Yah, who iss it?" he inquired.

A Minneapolis family discovered a nest of skunks under their house. After several attempts to get rid of the little stinkers had failed, they decided to ask some Norwegians down the street to bring some lutefisk to put under the house. The skunks left, all right. But then their problem was to get rid of the Norwegians.

A Swede and a Norwegian went up in a plane together. When the plane developed engine trouble, the two bailed out in parachutes. The Swede reached the ground in a matter of about a minute. But the Norwegian got lost and didn't get down until a half hour later.

Recently we heard about a Norwegian bookkeeper who absconded with the Accounts Payable.

What is it that's "Wet and Wild"?
A Norwegian with a stuck zipper.

Did you hear about the Norwegian girl who had a wooden baby?
Seems she got nailed by a carpenter.

Ordinarily "TGIF" means "Thank goodness it's Friday." Why do Norwegians have "TGIF" printed on their shoes?
It means "Toes go in first."

How do Norwegians spell "farm"?
"E-I-E-I-O"

LEVEL HEADED
NORWEGIAN

How can you identify a level headed Norwegian?
When the snoose runs out of both corners of his
his mouth.

What is the latest use for old garbage trucks?
The Norwegians make them into campers.

"Mission Impossible" is planning a special on TV.
Going to try to give a Norwegian a bath.

Teslow, the builder, had a Norwegian friend who died broke.
So, Teslow went out to raise some money for burial expenses.
"How about $10 to help bury a Norwegian," he asked Scott,
the lumber dealer. "Here's $100," said Scott. "Go bury 10 of
them."

They had to remove the speed bumps from the road
in our town. The Norwegians were trying to wash
clothes on them.

Did you hear about the man who was half Norwegian and half Japanese? Every December 7th, he goes out and attacks Pearl Olson.

At the Sons of Norway annual meeting, the treasure reported a deficit of $100. One of the Norwegians stood up and said, "I vote we donate half of it to the Red Cross and the other 75 to the Salvation Army."

We heard about a Norwegian who wanted to be a stud. So he had himself strapped to a snow tire.

What is a Norwegian dude?
One who has been circumcised with a pinking shears.

Two Norwegians from Minnesota went fishing in Canada. They caught one fish. When they got back, one of the Norwegians said, "The vay I figure our expenses, dat fish cost us $400." "Vell," said the other Norwegian, "at dat price, it's a good ting ve didn't catch any more."

Norwegian Christmas Card:
ABCDEFGHIJK MNOPQRSTUVWXYZ
(No L)

Two Norwegians bought a truck and went into the hay business. They travelled to Nebraska, buying hay for $1 a bale . . . they hauled it back to South Dakota where they sold it for $1 a bale. After a month or so, they did a little figuring and found out they were losing money. "Vell, dere's only vun ting to do," said one of the Norwegians. "Ve'll yust have to get us a bigger truck."

There was the Norwegian so dumb he thought a polaroid was a condition that came from sitting on the ice.

A Norwegian moved to Ireland and joined the IRA. His first assignment was to blow up a bus. But he failed because he burned his mouth on the exhaust pipe.

A Norwegian race driver entered the Indianapolis 500. He had to make 75 pit stops . . . 3 for gas and oil and tire changes and 72 to ask directions.

A Norwegian decided to take up hunting. So, off into the woods he went . . . when suddenly a beautiful blonde appeared. "Are you game?" asked the Norsky. "I certainly am, " purred the blonde. So the Norwegian shot her.

Did you hear about the Norwegian who could count to 10?
NO?
Would you believe FIVE?

HOW TO MAKE YOUR OWN NORWEGIAN FLASHLIGHT

1. TAKE THE CENTER TUBE FROM A ROLL OF TOILET PAPER.

2. USE CELLOPHANE TAPE TO BIND 12 PAPER MATCHES TO THE UPPER RIM OF TUBE.

3. TAPE STRIKER STRIP NEAR BOTTOM OF TUBE ALONG WITH STARTER MATCH!

Several Norwegian farmers from Minnesota, dissatisfied with low farm prices, decided to march on Washington. At last report, they were 15 miles south of Seattle.

Did you hear about the Norwegian who broke his shoulder during a milk drinking contest?
A cow fell on him.

A Norwegian in a hardware store asked if they had any burned out light bulbs.
He needed one for his photography darkroom.

Crop scientists have come up with a new strain known as "Norwegian Oats."
They are tall, light colored and empty headed.

A Norwegian noticed his car being stolen, so he chased it down the street trying to copy down the license number.

The Norwegian government has been having problems with their space program.
Their astronaut keeps falling off the kite.

Ever wonder who invented streaking?
It was a Norwegian who mistook Ben Gay for Preparation H.

Norwegian: Did you ever eat lutefisk?
Dane: No . . . but I think I stepped in some one time.

13

Why did the Norwegian sleep under an oil tank?
Because he wanted to get up oily.

Two Norwegians went with a pair of young ladies for a ride in the country. An hour later as Lars and Ole were trudging back to town on foot, Lars remarked, "Next time ve tell some girls to either cooperate or get out and valk . . . ve better make sure ve got our own car."

The phone company is going to pick a new emergency number to replace 911.
Most Norwegians can't find ELEVEN on the dial.

A Norwegian was having trouble picking a name for his new daughter. "I have trouble saying 'Yenevieve,' so I think we'll call her Wiolet."

A Norwegian thought diarrhea was hereditary because he discovered it in his genes (jeans).

What's the best thing to come out of Norway recently?
An empty boat.

There's a new Norwegian insurance policy. It's called "My Fault Insurance."

Lars: Vhere vould you find a turtle vid no legs?
Ole: Vell, I s'pose pretty much right vhere you left it.

What happens to Norwegians who can't tell putty from vaseline?
Their windows fall out.

A mathematics teacher moved to a Norwegian community where she attempted to teach the fundamentals of arithmetic and algebra. In an oral test one day, she asked Lars to explain "Pi R Squared." "Vell, teacher," said Lars. "You got it all wrong. Pie are round . . . it's corn bread which are square."

Two elderly Norwegian ladies in a nursing home decided one day to go "streaking" in order to relieve the monotony. As they paraded down the hallway in their all-together, two old codgers looked up from their wheelchairs. "What was that?" queried one of the old fellows. "Dunno," came the answer, "but whatever it was . . . it sure needed ironing."

New use for beer can tabs? "Combination Norwegian Wedding Ring and Nose Picker."

What was the smart thing the Norwegian did . . .
who had rented an outhouse to live in?
He sublet the basement to a Swede.

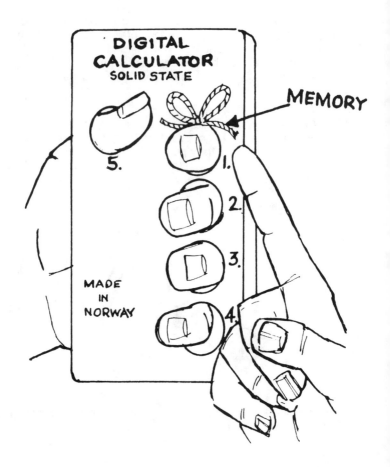

What was the tragedy concerning the four Norwegians who drowned in the station wagon that went into the river?
The wagon could have held 6.

What are the usual door prizes at a Norwegian wedding?
2nd prize: a night with the bride.
1st prize: 5 pounds of lutefisk.

A great medical breakthrough was recently reported.
The Norwegians have now performed the first successful hernia transplant.

Two Norwegians at the funeral of their friend Nels. "He sure looks good," said one. "He should," remarked the other, "He yust got out of the hospital."

Why do Norwegians have such pretty noses?
Because they're hand picked.

Who won the Norwegian beauty contest?
Nobody.

Two Norwegians were trying to get a mule into the barn but its ears were too long. One Norwegian suggested raising the barn. The other one thought they should dig a trench. "No, you dummy," exploded the first, "it's the ears that are too long, not the legs."

A Norwegian, when asked why he dragged a chain all over town, answered,
"Have you ever tried to push vun?"

3 most dangerous people in the world:
— An Irishman with a bottle of whiskey.
— A merchant with a box of matches.
— A Norwegian with a little education.

1st man: Do you know how to talk Norwegian?
2nd man: Nope . . . couldn't get the hang of it.
1st man: How does it feel to be DUMBER than a Norwegian?

On a recent charter plane trip from Minneapolis to Norway, the pilot was having difficulty maintaining the stability of his 747 jet. He learned from his co-pilot that a large bunch of Norwegians were aboard and they were creating quite a ruckus . . . imbibing a few spirits and running around the plane. So the co-pilot volunteered to go back to see if he could quiet them down. Shortly, the pilot was pleased to note the plane had settled down smoothly and he was able to resume on his course. When the co-pilot returned, the pilot asked how he managed to quiet down all those Norwegians. "It was easy," he said. "I just opened the rear hatch and told them there was free lutefisk in the basement."

Why does it cost $4 for a Norwegian to get a haircut?
One dollar per side.

What did the Norwegian call his mixture of prune juice and 7-Up?
"Hurry up."

Norwegian High Rise

Why does it take 5 Norwegians to paint a house?
You need one to hold the brush and 4 to turn the house.

A Norwegian answers the phone at 3 a.m. Wrong number, so the caller apologizes. "Dat's OK," said the Norwegian, "I had to get up to answer the phone anyway."

A Norwegian from Minnesota took a trip to Canada where he spied a well constructed pier out over a scenic lake. Said he, "I tink I'll build me vun just like it back in Minnesota." So, he got down on hands and knees to count the slats in order to have some idea how much lumber it would take. The Norwegian got so absorbed in counting slats that he tumbled right over the end of the pier into the water. Later, back on shore as he poured water from his pockets, boots, and ears, he was heard to mutter, "Vell, vun ting I found out. Ven you're out of Slats, you're out of Pier."

A landscaper was supervising a crew of Norwegians sodding a new lawn:
He had to keep shouting: "Green side up! Green side up!"

"Who invented the Limbo?"
A Norwegian trying to sneak under a pay toilet door.

What's black and blue and lies on the sidewalk?
The guy who tells too many Norwegian stories.

What happened to that Norwegian ice factory?
It had to close when they lost the recipe.

Describe a Norwegian marriage proposal.
"You're going to have a **WHAT**?"

How do they thin out the Norwegian population in Seattle?
They just throw a handful of coins out on the freeway.

We heard of a Norwegian who was so dumb he thought "innuendo" was the Italian word for Preparation H.

Describe a Norwegian Color TV.
A keyhole into the next apartment.

What has an IQ of 104?
Six Norwegians.

What did the Norwegian say when he saw his first pizza?
"Who trew up on da lefse?"

The Lutheran minister was chagrined because the church board denied his request for a chandelier for the church. When pressed for the reasons, the chairman explained to the preacher: "Vell, for vun ting . . . da secretary can't spell it. For anudder, nobody knows how to play it, so dat would be a vaste of money. And anudder ting . . . if ve are going to spend any money, it should be for a light over the pulpit so you can see better."

Who discovered Norway?
The Roto Rooter man.

A Norwegian, recently arrived in the U.S., was showing off his knowledge of the months of the year in English: "Yoon, You-lie, All-guts, Split timber, no vonder, all vinter."

Give an example of gross ignorance.
"144 Norwegians."

Then we heard about the Norwegian who cut down a big grove of trees with a chain saw. When he got through, someone showed him how to start the engine.

Describe a Norwegian compass.
A small mirror to show who's lost.

Then there was the Norwegian who went ice fishing. He brought back 50 pounds of ice, then he drowned trying to fry it.

What does R.S.V.P. mean on Norvegian wedding announcements?
"Remember . . . send Vedding present."

A Norwegian landed a job in a lumber yard. The first day they loaded 2 by 4's from a truck into a storage building. The foreman noticed that while the other men were carrying 4 timbers at a time, the Norwegian only carried one. When he politely asked the Norwegian why he carried only one at a time while the others carried 4, the Norwegian snorted, "I sure can't help it if dose odder guys are too lazy to make more trips."

What happened when the Norwegian library burned to the ground?
Both books were destroyed and one hadn't even been colored in.

Who was the dumbest Norwegian?
The one who thought Einstein was "one beer."

What are the three shortest books?
1. Book of Italian victories in WW II.
2. Irish book of etiquette.
3. Norwegian book of knowledge.

What did the Norwegian call his cocktail of Vodka and Milk of Magnesia?
"A Phillips Screwdriver."

Norwegian reading the Bible for the first time: "It says a lot about St. Paul but dere's notting in it about Minnoplis."

Norwegian Swing

"How does a Norwegian grease his car?"
He goes out and runs over an Italian.

What happened after the Norwegian lost a $50 bet
on a TV football play?
He lost another $50 on the instant replay.

1st Norsky: What's in the sack?
2nd Norsky: Chickens.
1st Norsky: How many?
2nd Norsky: If you can guess, I'll give you both of dem.

Who was the most famous Norwegian inventor?
Henry Fjord.

How did the Norwegian break his leg at the golf course?
He fell off the ball washer.

A Norwegian was strolling through the farm yard one day when he gazed down to find himself ankle deep in manure.
"Good heavens," he exclaimed. "I'm **MELTING!**"

A Norwegian took a trip to Fargo, North Dakota. While in a bar, an Indian on the next stool spoke to the Norwegian in a friendly manner. "Look," he said, "let's have a little game. I'll ask you a riddle. If you can answer it, I'll buy YOU a drink. If you can't then you buy ME one. OK?" "Yah, dat sounds purty good," said the Norwegian. Said the Indian, "My father and mother had one child, It wasn't my brother. It wasn't my sister. Who was it?" The Norwegian scratched his head and finally said, "I give up. Who vas it?" "It was ME," chortled the Indian. So the Norwegian paid for the drinks. Back in Sioux Falls the Norwegian went into a bar and spotted one of his cronies, Sven Sandvick. "Sven," he said, " I got a game. If you can answer a question, I'll buy YOU a drink. If you can't YOU buy Me vun. Fair enough? "Fair enough," said Sven. " OK . . . my father and mudder had vun child. It vasn't my brudder. It vasn't my sister. Who vas it?" "Search me?" said Sven. "I give up. Who was it?" Said the Norwegian, "It vas some Indian up in Fargo, North Dakota."

Why does it take 3 Norwegians to replace a light bulb?
One to hold the bulb and two to turn the ladder.

Norwegians are a different people in many ways. For instance, WHO but Norwegians would celebrate Easter by dying eggs WHITE.

NORWEGIAN SNO-MOBILE

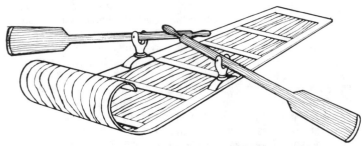

**SPECIAL DELUX MODEL
ONLY
$49.50 Plus Tax**

The little Norwegian boy gleefully reported to his dad after his first day at school. "What do you like best?" asked the Dad. "I like 'Gozinta' the best," said the little one. "Gozinta?" exclaimed the father . . . "What in the world is 'Gozinta'?" "Vell," said the youngster . . . "like 2 gozinta 4, 4 gozinta 8, and like that."

What did the Norwegian do with the Gold Medal he won at the Olympics?
He was so proud of it, he had it bronzed.

A Norwegian had a tough job sweeping up after the circus elephants. When asked why he didn't quit, he exclaimed, "What, and leave Show Biz?"

Define: "Dope ring."
Six Norwegians in a circle.

Do Norwegian teachers have ESP?
Yes. Extra simple pupils.

A Norwegian on his first plane ride. The pilot announced one engine had quit and the flight would be delayed a half hour. Later, another engine went out, and the pilot announced a one-hour delay. When a third engine went dead, the pilot announced a 90-minute delay. "My goodness," exclaimed the Norwegian, "If that last engine qvits, ve'll be up here all night!"

A Norwegian was hired to operated an elevator. But he lost his job after the first day. Couldn't learn the route.

A Norwegian carrying a rock, a chicken and a pail paused at a closed gate. He asked a Norwegian farm girl if she'd open the gate. She declined, saying, "You might make love to me." Snorted the Norsky, "How could I make love to you with a rock, a chicken and a pail in my arms?" "Vell," said the girl, "you could set the chicken down, put the pail over it, and then set the rock on top of the pail."

Ole Swenson was a painter. He had finished painting all the bedrooms upstairs and was to come back the next day and paint the downstairs rooms for Inga Olson. In the meantime, that eveing, her husband, Lars, came home a little tipsy, and while disrobing for bed, caught his foot in his pants leg and put his hand on the wall to steady himself. Of course he left a big smear.

Next day, Ole came to continue painting the downstairs. Inga met him at the door and said, "Ole, come up to the bedroom and see where my husband put his hand last night." Ole said, "No vay, Mrs. Olson. I came here to paint . . . not to fool around!"

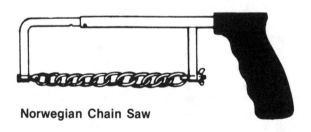

Norwegian Chain Saw

Last winter ten Norwegians were seen pushing a house down the street. They were trying to get the furnace started.

A NORWEGIAN MOTHER WRITING
TO HER SON

My dear son:

Yust a few lines to let yew know I am still alive. I am writing this letter slowly becoss I know you can't read fast.

You won't know the house when yew come home. Ve have moved.

Ve had a lot of trouble moving . . . especially the bed. The man vouldn't let us take it in the taxi. It maybe vouldn't have been so bad if your father hadn't been in it at the time.

Speaking of your father, he has a fine new yob. He has 500 men under him! (He cuts grass at the cemetery.)

Your sister got herself engaged last veek. Her boy friend gave her a beautiful ring with three stones missing.

Our neighbors are now raising pigs. Ve yust got vind of it this morning.

I suppose you didn't know I got my appendix out and a dish washer put in.

Ve found a vash machine in our new house . . . but it doesn't vork so good. Last veek I put in four shirts, pulled the chain and ve hasn't seen the shirts since.

Your sister Ingeborg had a baby yesterday. I haven't heard if it is a boy or a girl. So I can't say yet if you are an aunt or an uncle.

Uncle Thorvald vent to Minneapolis to vork in a bloomer factory. Ve hear he is pulling down 75 a week.

Your Aunt Katrina got a yob in St. Paul vorking in a factory, too. I'm sending her some clean underwear as she says she has been in the same shift since she got there.

Your father didn't have too much to drink at Christmas. I put some castor oil in his whiskey and it kept him going until New Years.

I vent to the doctor on Thursday. Your pa came with me. The Doctor put a glass tube in my mouth and said to keep it shut for ten minutes. Later on, your pa asked to buy it from him.

It vas so vindy last veek! On Monday it was so vindy, one of our chickens laid the same egg four times.

I must close now . . . there's a big sale down town and vomen's bloomers are half off.

Your loving Mother

p.s. I vas going to send you $10 but I already sealed the envelope.

There was a Norwegian in Minneapolis who was so dumb he thought "Johan pa Snippen" was a Swedish barber.

Swede: When I was in New York I contributed to the Atlantic Monthly.
Norwegian: That's nothing. When I was in California, I contributed to the Pacific daily.

The Norwegians have invented a new parachute. Opens on impact.

Why do Norwegian dogs have flat noses?
From chasing parked cars.

Why don't Nowegian mothers nurse their babies?
— Because it is so painful when they boil the nipple.

Why don't Norwegians play hide and seek?
'Cause nobody wants to find them.

The Norwegian was searching frantically for a half dollar when his friend strolled by. "Where'd ya lose it?" asked the friend.
"Over dere by my car," answered the Norwegian.
"Well, why don't you do your looking over by your car?"
"Because," said the Norsky, "da light is much better here."

Famous inventions: The Swedes invented the toilet seat. Twenty years later, the Norwegians invented the hole in it.

APPLICATION FOR MEMBERSHIP IN NORWEGIAN MOTORCYCLE CLUB "HELL'S NORSKYS"

Founded 1965 in Oslo [now in our 35th year]

Name . . . . av . . . . son

Nickname: . . . . Ole . . . . Lena . . . Oink . . . . Dummy . . . . Goof

Brand of Bike: . . . . Hondason; . . . . Triumphson; . . . . Skidooson;

. . . . Fordson; . . . . Yamahason; . . . . Kawasakison; . . . . Schwinnson.

Number of wheels: . . . 2; . . . . 3; . . . . 4; . . . . 5; Don't know

Shape of Wheels:
                    Round   Square   Oval   Other

Does bike have a side car? . . . . yes; . . . . no; . . . . Don't Know.

If yes, location of side car: . . . . front; . . . . rear.

Check style of club jacket desired:
. . . . Black leather with lefse on back.
. . . . Brown leather with lutefisk on back.
. . . . Tan leather with statue of Ole Bull on back.
. . . . Red and orange and purple and yellow and pink. (For weddings)
. . . . Skunk skin with dead Swede on back.
. . . . Do you want sleeves? If so, how many? . . . . 2; . . . . 3; . . . . none.

Your membership packet includes:
        Yellow babushka (reversable)
        Official Club training wheels
        Can of Cru-ex
        Tour ticket of Lutefisk plant
        One pair of sneakers

Dues: $15 per year ($1 per month)

Born: . . . . Citizen: Yes . . . . No . . . . Maybe . . . .

Married or single: Yes . . . . No . . . . Unknown . . . .

Sex: . . . . (Do not put down "occasionally")

Sex of wife (if known) . . . .

Age . . . . Unemployed fom what job? . . . .

Higher education (over 3rd grade) . . . .

Why don't the Norwegians tell Polish jokes?
— Because they don't understand them.

A Norwegian decided to drive to Omaha to see his cousin. About 20 miles from his destination, he saw a sign, "**OMAHA LEFT**." So he turned around and went back home.

A fellow in our hometown is starting a new business. He applies black paint on cement blocks and sells them to Norwegians as bowling balls.

A Norwegian in a bar spotted a good looking girl and told his friend, "I think I'll ask her for a date." "Naw," said the friend, "You don't want anything to do with her . . . she's a Lesbian." "Dat's OK," said the Norwegian as he ambled up to the Miss and asked, "Say, how are things in Beirut?"

About two centuries ago, the Swedes and the Norwegians were constantly at war with each other. During an invasion of Norway, the Swedish commander ordered his troops of 1,000 men to storm a Norwegian fort. A few minutes later, the Swedes dashed back in panic, "There were TWO Norwegians in that fort," they explained.

A Norwegian was brought to the hospital with severe facial burns. Seems he had been bobbing for French Fries.

I love to watch the Norwegian National Symphony between selections when they empty the saliva from their instruments. What's funny is that it's a string orchestra.

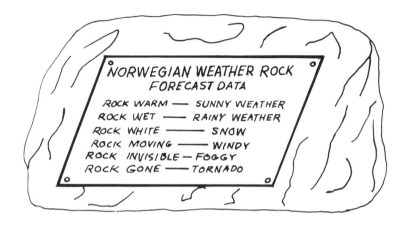

Make your own Norwegian Weather Rock

Why depend on unreliable TV forecasts?
Have your own never-fail method of determing the
weather.

Just find a suitable rock and put a label on it with
the information pictured above.

A Norwegian was fired at the local packing plant . . .
for putting brains in the Polish sausage.

What is two miles long and has an IQ of 6:
A Sons of Norway parade.

What do you call a 35 year old Norwegian in the
third grade?
A genius.

When the Norwegian accidentally lost 50 cents in the outhouse,
he immediately threw in his watch and billfold. He explained,
"I'm not going down dere yust for 50 cents."

During the big flood around Fargo in 1975, several
Norwegians waited by the river bank with
toothbrushes. They were waiting for the Crest.

A Norwegian came home one day and shot his dog. When a
neighbor expressed surprise, the Norwegian explained, "Some
vun phoned me up and said my vife was fooling around with
my best friend."

Then there was the Norwegian who noticed the sign,
"Wet Pavement" . . . so he did.

A Norwegian received a pair of water skis for his birthday.
He went crazy looking for a slope on the lake.

A Norwegian accidentally dropped his jacket into an outhouse. He was making quite a fuss so his compainion commented, "Why don't you forget it . . . it's an old jacket anyway." "I know it," said the Norwegian, "but I got my lunch in the pocket."

1st Norwegian: My brother's got a case of hemorrhoids.
2nd Norwegian: Svell. Let's go over and help him drink it.

Two Santa Clauses up on the roof. Which one is Norwegian? The one with the Easter Basket.

Back in the pioneer days there was a Norwegian settler named Ole. He built his family a nice cabin, and then commenced to till the soil. For his family's safety, Ole installed a large bell, instructing his wife to ring it if an extreme emergency arose. The next week, Ole heard the bell ringing, so he grabbed his rifle and ran madly to the house. There was Lena, fetching one of the youngsters out of the well. Ole was furious because he didn't consider it a dire emergency. A few days later, Ole was again summoned by the ringing bell. When he got to the house, Ole breathlessly asked what the trouble was. "Oh, da cows got into da corn," explained Lena. Again, Ole was furious, chastising his wife for calling him home on such a flimsy "emergency." About a week later, Ole again heard the clanging bell. But this time he took his time, finishing up a row he'd been plowing. As he leisurely strolled home, he stopped briefly to pick some blueberries. Then, as he came over a hill, he saw his home in flames. All the livestock had been slaughtered, and his wife and children wounded. As he gazed on the scene, Ole was heard to comment: "Velll...DAT'S more like it!"

A—Norwegian Ambush
B—Norwegian Weather Report
(Tree Below Zero)
C—Norwegian Quarter Pounder

What does a Norwegian say when he picks his nose?
Grace.

A Norwegian fox became caught in a trap. It chewed off three of its feet only to find out it was still caught.

How do you identify the bride at a Norwegian wedding?
She's the one with the braided armpits.

How do you break a Norwegian's finger?
Punch him in the nose.

What is a big awkward animal with a trunk?
A Norwegian on vacation.

What is the Norwegian national anthem?
"Shoo Fly Don't Bother me."

What is a Norwegian shishkabob?
A flaming arrow through a garbage can.

What is a Norwegian called who chases garbage trucks?
"A galloping gourmet."

Why do they bury Norwegians with their rear ends sticking out of the ground?
So they can be used for bicycle racks.

How can it be proved that Adam was a Norwegian?
Who else would stand beside a naked woman and
just eat an apple?

Why are Norwegian mothers so strong?
From raising dumb-bells.

Why were wheelbarrows invented?
To teach the Norwegians to walk on their hind legs.

There once was a Norwegian who, in a rage, flung himself upon
the floor. And missed.

A Norwegian butcher backed into the meat grinder
and got a little behind in his work.

Two Norwegians opened a bank. After loaning out all the money,
they skipped town.

Customer: "Do you have the book, 'The Smart
Norwegian'?"
Bookstore Clerk: "Yes. It's in the fiction
department."

There was a Norwegian so lazy that he married a pregnant
woman.

Why do flies have wings?
So they can beat the Norwegians to the garbage
cans.

A cannibal was checking out prices at his local meat market. He asked the vendor why the Irishman cost 90 cents a pound, the German 85 cents a pound and the Norwegian was priced $1.50 per pound. "Why does the Norwegian cost so much?" he asked. "Well," came the answer, "did you ever try to clean one?"

Two Norwegian brothers kept their two horses in a pasture. To tell them apart, they trimmed the tail on one horse. Later, they discovered the black horse was about 8 inches shorter than the white one.

A Norwegian arrived in California two weeks late on his trip from Fargo. He explained the delay. "Vell, I kept seeing those signs 'Clean Rest Rooms,' so I had to clean 400 on the way out."

Norwegian Tying His Shoe

A Norwegian lady quit using the pill.
Kept falling out.

Lady (attending the Olympics): "Are you a Pole Vaulter?"
Norwegian: "No . . . I'm a Norwegian . . . and my name ain't Valter."

A TV network is planning a two hour special. A Norwegian will attempt to count to 100.

Woman: Oh, my goodness . . . my husband is driving in the driveway!
Norwegian: I better get outta here. Vhere is your back door?
Woman: We don't have a back door.
Norwegian: Vell, vhere vould you like vun?

Did you hear about the intelligent Norwegian?
It was just a rumor.

Why does it take two Norwegians to make chocolate chip cookies?
One to mix the batter and one to squeeze the rabbit.

A Norwegian girl competed with a French girl and an English girl in the Breast Stroke division of an English Channel swim competition. The French girl came in first, the English girl second. The Norwegian girl reached shore completely exhausted. After being revived with blankets and coffee, she remarked, "I don't vant to complain, but I tink those other two girls used their arms."

GENUINE NORWEGIAN WOOD STOVE

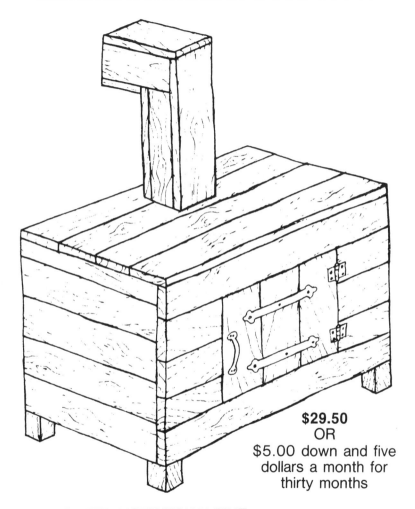

$29.50
OR
$5.00 down and five
dollars a month for
thirty months

★ IMPORTED NORWEGIAN PINE
★ FIREPROOF, REUSABLE BRASS FIXTURES
★ GUARANTEED TO BURN OR YOUR MONEY BACK

Two Norwegians went deer hunting when one of them accidentally shot the other. The victim was finally taken to the hospital where the Doctors labored to save him. As the other Norwegian paced out in the lobby, the Doctor came out and said, "He was pretty badly shot . . . but I think we might have been able to save him if you hadn't dressed him out."

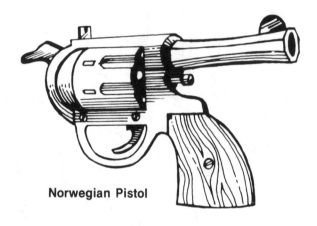

Norwegian Pistol

Two Norwegians were building a house. One of them reached into a sack of nails and said, "Lars, you got us the wrong kind of nails. Dese nails have got the point on the wrong end."
"Dat's okay," said Lars. "Ve can use dem on the other side of the house."

A Norwegian in Minneapolis moved his house back 50 feet to take up the slack in his clothes line.

Why don't they allow Norwegians to swim in Lake Superior?
Because they leave a ring.

What happened to the Norwegian who ate the Gammelost? (Old cheese)
They tipped him over 4 times on Halloween.

A German, an Italian and a Norwegian were trying to get ito the stadium at the World Olympics at Montreal, but the seats were all sold out. The enterprising German stripped down to his shorts and undershirt, picked up a cane fishing pole in a nearby alley, and marched right in, stating boldly, "Heinrich Schneider, Germany, Pole Vault."
Noting the successful ploy, the Italian took off his outer garments, grabbed a large round stone, then just as boldly strode in the gate, announcing, "Pasquale Galento, Italy, Shot Put."
Not to be outdone, the Norwegian took off all but his BVD's, went into a nearby hardware store where he purchased some barbed wire. As he approached the gate the Norwegian spoke out confidently, "Hjalmar Olson, Norvay, fencing."

Two Swedes and two Norwegians went ice fishing. The Norwegians stood at their spot for about an hour with no results. One of them walked a hundred yards to where the Swedes stood with a big string of fish. Going back to his partner, the Norwegian reported on the huge catch by the Swedes. "What are they doing different?" asked the first Norwegian. "Vell," said the second, "for one ting they cut a hole in the ice."

TWO NORWEGIANS WALKING ABREAST

Two Norwegians were hired at a Lady's Underwear factory in Minneapolis. The first pay day, they compared paychecks. Ole discovered that Knute was paid $11 an hour, while he, Ole, received only $4.50. So he went to the personnel manager and complained about the wide variance in pay. "Well," said the company man, "Knute told us he had eleven years experience in Norway as a Diesel Fitter, while you show on your application only 4½ years as a Crotch Sewer." "Yah . . . dat's true," said Ole. "But Yimminy Christmas, look at the difference in the vork. I vork all day sewing in the crotches of da lady's undervear. Den Knute . . . all he has to do is hold 'em up, look 'em over and say, "Yah, dese'll fit her."

A Norwegian whose wife was expecting twins had to go on a trip. He asked his brother to name the off-spring when they arrived. Upon his return, he asked the brother what names he had given the new twins. "Da girl is Da-neese," explained the brother. "Denise? Nice name . . . and the boy?" asked the father. Replied the brother: "Da Nephew."

The Swedes are proud of their new zoo.
They built a fence around Norway.

Two Norwegians were talking in the park when a bird splattered one of them on the head. Eyeing the mess, the victim's companion offered to go get some toilet paper. "Von't do no good," said the messed-up one, "by the time you get back, dat bird will be four miles avay."

There once was a Norwegian Kamakaze pilot who managed to rack up 25 suicide missions.

Why do Norwegians smile when it lightnings?
They think they're getting their picture taken.

Woman: I was just raped by a Norwegian.
Policeman: How do you know he was Norwegian?
Woman: I had to show him how.

Did you hear about the Norwegian who had his bathroom carpeted?
He liked it so well that he had it carpeted all the way to the house.

Describe a Norwegian garbage disposal.

A pig under the sink.

Lena lay dying, and on her deathbed she decided to make a confession. "Ole, I have to confess to you before I go dat I vas unfaithful to you."
'Dat's OK, Lena," answered Ole. "I have a confession to make, too. It vas me dat poisoned you."

What is this?

A Norwegian handkerchief

And these:

Norwegian silverware

There's even MORE fun waiting when you order from the book list below.

	Price	Qty.	Total
* Polish Jokes	$3.00		
* Norwegian Jokes	$3.00		
* Uff Da Jokes	$3.00		
* Ole & Lena Jokes 1	$3.00		
* More Ole & Lena Jokes 2	$3.00		
* Ole & Lena Jokes III	$3.00		
* Ole & Lena Jokes 4	$3.00		
* Ole & Lena Jokes 5	$3.00		
* Ole & Lena Jokes 6	$3.00		
* Ole & Lena Jokes 7	$3.00		
* Office Jokes (R Rated)	$2.75		
* Blonde Jokes	$2.50		
* Norwegian Book of Knowledge	$1.75		
(Above title has blank text and humorous material on back cover)			
* How to Become Your Own Boss ... Shortcuts on becoming self-employed	$4.95		
GRAND TOTAL			

ALL PRICES INCLUDE POSTAGE AND HANDLING
10% DISCOUNT ON ORDERS OVER $15.00

Name _____

Address _____

_____

Send check or money order to:
NORSE PRESS, Box 1554, Sioux Falls, SD 57101

47